For Ella, Elizabeth and Rory, future HR Superstars

What bedtime story would you like tonight?

I would like a story about your **job**... and a funfair...with my favourite animals of course...and don't forget **Goldie**!

Mummy works in **Human Resources** in a big office.
Mummy has to **find people** to do all the jobs that need to be done.

And also, to make sure everybody is doing a job they are **good** at.

Mummy talks to colleagues in far-away places to **share ideas**.

Some days, Mummy **teaches new skills** to people at work, so they can do different jobs.

Other days, Mummy does not see anybody at work, she is too busy **writing reports** for the big bosses.

When somebody at work is naughty,
it is Mummy's job to tell them off.
Everyone at work must be **fair** to each other
or we may ask them to go home.

Mummy also has happy conversations, like when somebody does a good job, Mummy gives them praise and gives them a **reward.**

Mummy has to make sure work is a
fun place to be,
but also a safe place.

Some jobs can be hard work, so Mummy makes sure everyone gets the **rest** they need to stay fit and healthy.

Mummy does **coaching** to help everyone reach their goals and perform at their best.

Mummy helps everyone to be friends
and **work together** to get the jobs done.

The favourite part of my day though, is coming home to **you** and telling bedtime stories.

GLOSSARY

TALENT ACQUISITION
is the process of finding, attracting and assessing (through interviews) talent to join your company.

LEARNING & DEVELOPMENT
is a system to improve the skills and knowledge of employees to improve their future performance.

NETWORKING/BENCHMARKING
is the action of interacting with others to exchange information and develop professional contacts.

DISCIPLINE
is the set of conditions imposed on employees by management in order to prevent employees doing anything detrimental to the company. It establishes standards of job performanc and encourages employees to behave sensibly and safely at work.

FUN
workplaces create an environment that enhances learning, productivity and creativity while reducing employee burnout and absenteeism. It shows appreciation for the time and effort employees give to the organization.

REWARD

is an incentive plan to reinforce the desirable behavior of workers or employers and in return for their service to the organization. By offering rewards, companies can attract, maintain and retain efficient, high performing and motivated employees.

TEAM BONDING

is the process of turning a group of individuals into a cohesive and effective team.

REPORTING

provides data on people and performance to make informed decisions.

HEALTH & WELLBEING

supporting both physical and mental wellbeing through office design can help create a healthy and productive workforce.

COACHING

is a process that is designed to assist motivated individuals in making changes to further develop their personal development.

ORGANISATION DESIGN

is the process of aligning structure and roles at a company to the objectives, with the aim of improving efficiency and effectiveness.

The **End**

More about MummyBooks

Unless you are an astronaut or a nurse it can be hard to explain to your children just what you do all day at work and why it is important.

There are few role model office jobs, so this series of books is designed to tell the story through the eyes of children what mummy does at work.

We start by using non-human resources in the form of our favourite animals to explain the role of Human Resources. The first in an engaging series of books which will be enjoyed by children and parents alike.

Check us out at mummybooks.com

Made in United States
North Haven, CT
07 February 2023

32167466R00020